Why the HOLY SPIRIT?

EXPERIENCING GOD'S PURPOSE AND PLAN
FOR HIS SPIRIT IN YOUR LIFE

JENTEZEN FRANKLIN

Why the Holy Spirit?
Experiencing God's Purpose and Plan for His Spirit In Your Life

Published 2015 by Jentezen Franklin Media Ministries, Gainesville, GA
A Jentezen Franklin Media Ministries Publication

ISBN: 978-0-9833264-4-1

Editing/Graphic Design by Roark Creative
www.roarkcreative.com

Jentezen Franklin Media Ministries
P.O. Box 315
Gainesville, GA 30503
888-333-0049

jentezenfranklin.org

Printed and bound in the United States of America.

Why the HOLY SPIRIT?

EXPERIENCING GOD'S PURPOSE AND PLAN
FOR HIS SPIRIT IN YOUR LIFE

CONTENTS

Introduction	9
Chapter 1: What or *Who* is the Holy Spirit?	15
Chapter 2: When did the Holy Spirit arrive?	25
Chapter 3: Why do we need the Holy Spirit?	33
Chapter 4: How do I receive the Holy Spirit?	41
Chapter 5: How does the Holy Spirit work in our lives?	49
Chapter 6: Is the Holy Spirit still at work today?	59

And we are his witnesses of these things; and so is also the Holy Ghost, whom God hath given to them that obey him.

– Acts 5:32

INTRODUCTION

Mysteries of the Holy Spirit Revealed!

If the Holy Spirit is a mystery to you, you are not alone. I cannot tell you how many times I've been asked questions like:

What is the Holy Spirit?

How do I receive the Holy Spirit?

Do Christians really need the Holy Spirit today?

The truth is that the Holy Spirit should not be a mystery to any believer ... He is a person equal in every way with God the Father and God the Son.

He, whose role is clearly explained in Scripture, is an integral part of our walk of faith.

God sent His Spirit to be our Comforter and Encourager!

The Holy Spirit connects us to God ... reveals truth ... teaches us ... empowers us ... protects and encourages us ... and so much more.

Jesus gave specific instruction on the power and purpose of the Holy Spirit.

"I have yet many things to say unto you, but ye cannot bear them now. Howbeit when he, the Spirit of truth, is come, he will guide you into all truth: for he shall not speak of himself; but whatsoever he shall hear, that shall he speak: and he will shew you things to come. He shall glorify me: for he shall receive of mine, and shall shew it unto you" (John 16:12-15).

God's Word shares the identity, purpose, and plan for the Holy Spirit on this earth. And I can tell you from personal experience . . . when you receive the Holy Spirit, your life will never be the same!

I've written this book to help answer questions many people have asked me regarding the incredible gift and power that the Holy Spirit provides.

I want you to experience the power of the Holy Spirit in your daily life. And I pray this book serves as an eye-opening guide into God's divine plan to fill your life with His presence through the person of the Holy Spirit.

I encourage you to meditate on the Scriptures in this book and then pray that God will fill you to overflowing with His Spirit!

"Now the God of hope fill you with all joy and peace in believing, that ye may abound in hope, through the power of the Holy Ghost."
– Romans 15:13

Howbeit when he, the Spirit of truth, is come, he will guide you into all truth: for he shall not speak of himself; but whatsoever he shall hear, that shall he speak: and he will shew you things to come.

—John 16:13

CHAPTER 1

What or Who is the Holy Spirit?

If you want to experience all that God has provided for you, then living with the power and walking in the confidence of the Holy Spirit is a must. But too often, even a mention of the Holy Spirit raises eyebrows of confusion. Why?

Sometimes, it is simply a matter of people failing to understand God's purpose for the Holy Spirit in our lives. Everyone has an opinion, but the facts found in God's Word are without doubt. Let's unravel the mystery of the Third Person of the Trinity!

First, we can shine some light on exactly "Who" the Holy Spirit is.

The Holy Spirit is God's promise for comfort, power, truth, and so much more. Jesus said,

"If ye love me, keep my commandments. And I will pray the Father, and he shall give you another Comforter, that he may abide with you forever; Even the Spirit of truth; whom the world cannot receive, because it seeth him not, neither knoweth him: but ye know him; for he dwelleth with you, and shall be in you" (John 14:15-17).

Did you catch that . . . He lives in you!

The Holy Spirit is a real person; the third person of the Godhead: The Holy Trinity—the Father, the Son, and the Holy Ghost—are referenced several times in Scripture:

"For there are three that bear record in heaven, the Father, the Word, and the Holy Ghost: and these three are one" (1 John 5:7).

"Go ye therefore, and teach all nations, baptizing them in the name of the Father, and of the Son, and of the Holy Ghost" (Matthew 28:19).

"And Jesus, when he was baptized, went up straightway out of the water: and, lo, the heavens were opened unto him, and he saw the Spirit of God descending like a dove, and lighting upon him: And lo a voice from heaven, saying, This is my beloved Son, in whom I am well pleased" (Matthew 3:16-17).

The Holy Spirit is not an "it" . . . He's a person!

The Holy Spirit is God's Presence "in" you. Under the old covenant God was with Daniel, Ezekiel, Isaiah, Elisha, and Elijah during incredible, miraculous moments in history. But under the new covenant, through the Holy Spirit, God chooses to live in us!

In the church, we believe in Bethlehem's manger. We believe in Calvary's cross and Jesus' resurrection on the third day. But when we discuss the Upper Room, it is as if religion tries to slam that door shut.

Bethlehem was God with us. Calvary was God for us. But Pentecost is God in us!

The Holy Spirit is our Heavenly communicator.

The Spirit of the Lord knows how to usher us into God's presence through praise and worship. There are spiritual dimensions that we will never realize without the help of the intercessor—the Spirit of God. One of the communication tools used by the Holy Spirit is that of speaking in tongues.

"For he that speaketh in an [unknown] tongue speaketh not unto men, but unto God: for no man understandeth [him]; howbeit in the spirit he speaketh mysteries" (1 Corinthians 14:2).

> "And these signs shall follow them that believe; In my name shall they cast out devils; they shall speak with new tongues."
> – Mark 16:17

Simply put, the Holy Spirit's presence in me gives me the language to speak directly to God.

The Holy Spirit is the great Comforter.

Jesus often referred to the Holy Spirit as the Comforter. "Nevertheless I tell you the truth; It is expedient for you that I go away: for if I go not away, the Comforter will not come unto you; but if I depart, I will send him unto you. And when he is come, he will reprove the world of sin, and of righteousness, and of judgment" (John 16:7-8).

The Holy Spirit offers encouragement and guidance right when we need it the most!

We're living in a time when people need a demonstration of the power of the Holy Spirit. We're living in an age when the Church needs an awakening to the importance of being filled with the Holy Ghost.

God has blessed us to live under the new covenant, not the old covenant. One of the mighty blessings of the new covenant is the power of the Holy Spirit, the baptism in the Holy Spirit, and the presence of the Holy Spirit living here with us and in us on a permanent basis. He isn't some mystical force. In scripture He is portrayed as a dove, so don't ever be afraid of the Holy Spirit and what He will do to you.

The Flight of the Dove

Jesus knew the importance of His own baptism as He began His public ministry.

That is why He sought out John the Baptist. When He obeyed God, He was strengthened and anointed by the power of the Holy Spirit

"Then cometh Jesus from Galilee to Jordan unto John, to be baptized of him.

But John forbad him, saying, I have need to be baptized of thee, and comest thou to me?

And Jesus answering said unto him, Suffer it to be so now: for thus it becometh us to fulfill all righteousness. Then he suffered him.

And Jesus, when he was baptized, went up straightway out of the water: and, lo, the heavens were opened unto him, and he saw the Spirit of God descending like a dove, and lighting upon him:

And lo a voice from heaven, saying, This is my beloved Son, in whom I am well pleased" (Matthew 3:13-17).

When you see the dove, it is representative of the Holy Spirit.

And such were some of you: but ye are washed, but ye are sanctified, but ye are justified in the name of the Lord Jesus, and by the Spirit of our God.

— 1 Corinthians 6:11

CHAPTER 2

When did the Holy Spirit arrive?

As part of the Godhead, the Holy Spirit has been around from the beginning. "In the beginning God created the heaven and the earth. And the earth was without form, and void; and darkness was upon the face of the deep. And the spirit of God moved upon the face of the waters" (Genesis 1:1-2).

The Bible refers to visitations from the Holy Spirit on earth throughout the Old Testament.

An example is found in Numbers 11:25 when God anointed elders to give Moses relief. "And the Lord came down in a cloud, and spake unto him, and took of the spirit that was upon him, and gave it unto the seventy elders: and it came to pass, that, when the spirit rested upon them, they prophesied, and did not cease". This visitation was a foretaste of how God would pour out His Spirit in later days.

The Spirit also descended upon Samson, gave him strength, and then lifted. The Spirit rested upon Gideon and David. Each one experienced a temporary anointing of the Holy Spirit to carry out God's purpose, whether to defeat armies or giants.

There are only eight occasions in the Old Testament that the Spirit was "in" men and twenty-five when the Holy Spirit came "upon" men.

Jesus promised that the Holy Spirit would descend upon the earth for everyone and remain after His death and resurrection.

> "Howbeit when he, the Spirit of truth, is come, he will guide you into all truth: for he shall not speak of himself; but whatsoever he shall hear, that shall he speak: and he will shew you things to come." – John 16:13

"But the Comforter, which is the Holy Ghost, whom the Father will send in my name, he shall teach you all things, and bring all things to your remembrance,

> "Then said Jesus to them again, Peace be unto you: as my Father hath sent me, even so send I you. And when he had said this, he breathed on them, and saith unto them, Receive ye the Holy Ghost."
> – John 20:21-22

whatsoever I have said unto you" (John 14:26).

God's promise was fulfilled on the Day of Pentecost!

"And when the day of Pentecost was fully come, they were all with one accord in one place. And suddenly there came a sound from heaven as of a rushing mighty wind, and it filled all the house where they were sitting. And there appeared unto them cloven tongues like as of fire, and it sat upon each of them. And they were all filled with the Holy Ghost, and began to speak with other tongues, as the Spirit gave them utterance" (Acts 2:1-4).

In this moment, the power of the Holy Spirit was unleashed onto the earth to do the full-time ministry of Jesus Christ and the Father through believers.

It was not only a promise kept, but a prophecy fulfilled! ◆

"But this is that which was spoken by the prophet Joel; And it shall come to pass in the last days, saith God, I will pour out of my Spirit upon all flesh: and your sons and your daughters shall prophesy, and your young men shall see visions, and your old men shall dream dreams: And on my servants and on my handmaidens I will pour out in those days of my Spirit; and they shall prophesy . . . And it shall come to pass, that whosoever shall call on the name of the Lord shall be saved" (Acts 2:16-18,21).

And not only so, but we glory in tribulations also: knowing that tribulation worketh patience;

And patience, experience; and experience, hope:

And hope maketh not ashamed; because the love of God is shed abroad in our hearts by the Holy Ghost which is given unto us.

– Romans 5:3-5

CHAPTER 3

Why do we need the Holy Spirit?

I love telling a story that I read in the LA Times.

Los Angeles, California city officials commissioned an environmental expert to extensively study and solve L.A.'s pollution problem.

After much deliberation, the day arrived for the press conference and release of the research findings. City officials and special guests gathered in anticipation.

The expert stood at the microphone and admitted, "I'm embarrassed to give this report, knowing you paid a large sum of money for our findings.

Honestly, there is no solution for your pollution problem. We really just need a wind from elsewhere to sweep through your city, blowing pollution to the sea and cleansing your city!"

Being a preacher, I think that story perfectly illustrates the power of the Holy Spirit . . . a wind from elsewhere!

Before Christ came, God's relationship with His people had been polluted by sin.

In Acts 2 the Holy Spirit descended upon the disciples like a "rushing mighty wind" in the Upper Room.

> "And suddenly there came a sound from heaven as of a rushing mighty wind, and it filled all the house where they were sitting."
> – Acts 2:2

The Holy Spirit swept out dead religion and brought joy to their hearts. The mighty wind of the Holy Spirit came straight from Heaven, pushed out the fog of sin, brought power and anointing, changing men like Peter who had cursed and denied Jesus.

The wind removed fear and uncertainty, empowering Peter and others to speak Words of Life with boldness.

> "But ye shall receive power, after that the Holy Ghost is come upon you: and ye shall be witnesses unto me both in Jerusalem, and in all Judaea, and in Samaria, and unto the uttermost part of the earth."
> — Acts 1:8

They became powerful witnesses of Jesus.

"But ye shall receive power, after that the Holy Ghost is come upon you: and ye shall be witnesses unto me both in Jerusalem, and in all Judaea, and in Samaria, and unto the uttermost part of the earth" (Acts 1:8).

We need a fresh encounter today with the mighty wind of the Holy Spirit!

We need the Holy Spirit to sweep through our hearts, through our families, through our churches, through our cities, through our schools, through our courts, and through the governments of our nation.

Only the Holy Spirit can sweep away sin, prejudice, marriage troubles, addictions, and iniquity . . . and bring life, joy, and peace!

In Ezekiel 37 the Spirit of the LORD came upon Ezekiel

and set him in the midst of a valley, full of dry bones.

God empowered Ezekiel to breathe life into the bones. ". . . So I prophesied [live] as He commanded me, and breath came into them, and they lived, and stood upon their feet . . ." (Ezekiel 37:1-10).

The Bible said that the wind began to blow and the dry bones—I love the wording—"stood on their feet".

I believe the mighty wind of the same Holy Spirit that swept through that valley can also breathe life into what seems beyond repair in your life.

Maybe you think you've gone too far into sin. Maybe divorce knocked you off of your feet. Maybe you've fallen into that same addiction again. Maybe financial devastation left you hopeless.

Hell says, "You're down for the count. You will never get on your feet again."

I want to tell you that you can get back on your feet when the wind from elsewhere comes. He will pick you up. The Holy Spirit will put the pieces back together. Sometimes man's best efforts can't fix your problem. But if the wind from elsewhere starts blowing, He can get you back on your feet again.

"It's not by might, it's not by power, it's by My Spirit" (Zechariah 4:6). "This Wind From Elsewhere" . . . "The

Holy Spirit" . . . will cause you to pray, to love God, to read your Bible, to be passionate for Jesus, and to live right.

No matter what else you need today, your greatest need is a wind from elsewhere . . . The Holy Spirit!

The Holy Spirit offers so many benefits to believers! According to Romans 8, three specific ways the Holy Spirit can help you grow in your walk of faith are:

First, when the Holy Spirit comes into your life, He will confirm to you that you are a child of God.

Secondly, the Holy Spirit will lead you into God's purpose and plan for your life.

Third, He will quicken your mortal body. The Holy Spirit can quicken your health. He can renew your body and your mind, like no other!

I indeed baptize you with water unto repentance. but he that cometh after me is mightier than I, whose shoes I am not worthy to bear: he shall baptize you with the Holy Ghost, and with fire:

— Matthew 3:11

CHAPTER 4

How do you receive the Holy Spirit?

The most important event that has happened for mankind since Calvary is Pentecost. But the most important question today is: Has it happened to you?

Jesus said, "He that believeth on me, as the scripture hath said, out of his belly shall flow rivers of living water" (John 7:38).

When the Holy Spirit fills you, He lives and dwells in you.

How amazing that we can become a "temple" or a "vessel" for God's Spirit to flow!

Before you can flow with living water, however, you must be an empty vessel who wants more of

God. A successful career is not required … material possessions are not enough! We are just empty vessels without the Holy Spirit.

"Blessed are they which do hunger and thirst after righteousness: for they shall be filled" (Matthew 5:6) Are you hungry today? If so, Scripture outlines the plan to receive the Holy Spirit.

"Then Peter said unto them, Repent, and be baptized every one of you in the name of Jesus Christ for the remission of sins, and ye shall receive the gift of the Holy Ghost" (Acts 2:38).

The first step is to repent and confess your sins.

Ask for forgiveness and you will receive it. Once your temple is purified by God's grace, the Holy Spirit can dwell in you.

"Know ye not that ye are the temple of God, and that the Spirit of God dwelleth in you? (1 Corinthians 3:16).

Once you are prepared, follow the example of the disciples. They gathered together for prayer and to wait on God's gift.

Three essential ingredients!

When you baptize someone in the natural, water baptism, there are three things that must be present:

1. There must be a baptizer—the pastor.
2. There must be a person presenting him or herself to be baptized.
3. And there must be an element into which they are being baptized called water.

The same is true for the Baptism in the Holy Spirit. There must be a Baptizer, Jesus said. There must be people who present themselves to be baptized. And there must be an element into which they are baptized, and that is the Holy Ghost!

Prayer and worship, welcome the Holy Spirit.

"And when they had prayed, the place was shaken where they were assembled together; and they were all filled with the Holy Ghost, and they spake the word of God with boldness" (Acts 4:31).

If we follow His commands, God is faithful!

"For the promise is unto you, and to your children, and to all that are afar off, even as many as the Lord our God shall call" (Acts 2:39).

Following in Mary's footsteps

Jesus' virgin birth was made possible by the Holy Spirit.

"Then said Mary unto the angel, How shall this be, seeing I know not a man? And the angel answered and said unto her, The Holy Ghost shall come upon thee, and the power of the Highest shall overshadow thee: therefore also that holy thing which shall be born of thee shall be called the Son of God" (Luke 1:34-35).

What made God choose Mary for such a critical assignment?

Why did He send the Holy Spirit to work in her life?

- She had a "virgin" spirit. When God wants to birth something in someone, He looks for purity. Mary had a pure heart. God used someone who stood out in their lifestyle and integrity.

- She beleived and God spoke to her. Mary never doubted that God could accomplish what He said, she just asked how. God will send the Holy Spirit to overtake you when you refuse to put Him in a box. When God is ready to do something on this earth, He looks for people who are open!

Follow in Mary's footsteps and be ready for God to work a miracle through the Holy Spirit in you!

But the fruit of the Spirit is love, joy, peace, longsuffering, gentleness, goodness, faith, Meekness, temperance: against such there is no law.

— Galatians 5:22-23

CHAPTER 5

How does the Holy Spirit work in our lives?

The Holy Spirit continues God's work here on earth that began with Jesus. From the moment the dove landed on Jesus' head after His baptism, His public ministry began—full of redemption, power, healing, miracles, and more.

Jesus said, "The Spirit of the Lord is upon me, because he hath anointed me to preach the gospel to the poor; he hath sent me to heal the brokenhearted, to preach deliverance to the captives, and recovering of sight to the blind, to set at liberty them that are bruised" (Luke 4:18).

What does that have to do with my everyday life, you ask? Everything!

When the Holy Spirit fills you, the Holy Spirit is enough. He is your Healer. He is your Deliverer. He is your Help. He is your Answer. He is the Revealer of secrets.

The Holy Spirit provides:

POWER

Romans 8 teaches how the Holy Spirit empowers God's people to succeed. The Bible says, "Likewise the Spirit also helpeth our infirmities" (Romans 8:26). The Spirit stands alongside as our ally. He's waiting in the wings, ready and willing to help us when we're in trouble.

The key to victory is through the power of the Holy Spirit! How will you save your marriage? The Holy Spirit! How will you overcome an addiction or know your children are safe in God's care? The Holy Spirit!

DREAMS AND VISIONS

Proverbs 29:18 says, "Where there is no vision, the people perish: but he that keepeth the law, happy is he." God wants you to have a vision and a dream . . . one that the Holy Spirit gives you.

Joel prophesied that when God pours out His Spirit, "young men shall see visions, and your old men shall dream dreams" (Acts 2:17).

The Holy Spirit gives us dreams and guides our lives toward that vision. And even better news is that God's plans are bigger than you could ever imagine.

FREEDOM

Has fear, a dark past, or some other vice bound you?

The Holy Spirit is the key to the freedom you want. He's waiting in the wings as an ally, ready and willing to help you when you're in trouble. When I'm at work or in a situation and am unable to produce results, my ally is waiting in the wings and He says, "Not by might, nor by power, but by my spirit, saith the Lord of hosts" (Zechariah 4:6).

PRAYER LANGUAGE

Through the Holy Spirit, you pray and the enemy cannot even understand! "For he that speaketh in an unknown tongue speaketh not unto men, but unto God: for no man understandeth him; howbeit in the spirit he speaketh mysteries" (1 Corinthians 14:2).

Praying in the Holy Ghost is a powerful spiritual weapon that you need to use daily. Praying in the Spirit coats you with the armor of God—from the top of your head, to the soles of your feet. When you pray in the Spirit, you suit up spiritually and equip yourself to defeat the devil and destroy his power.

Whether you know what you need to pray for or not, the Holy Spirit knows. He makes intercession on your behalf before the Father.

> ". . . for we know not what we should pray for as we ought: but the Spirit itself maketh intercession for us with groanings which cannot be uttered"
> — Romans 8:26

When you pray in the Holy Ghost, He also imparts supernatural discernment.

It's a feeling deep down inside you that gives you peace about what you are praying for!

He makes intercession for you. He knows the mind of the Father about every area for your life. When you pray in the Holy Ghost, He injects a supernatural feeling inside you that translates into having, or not having, peace about your decisions.

God uses the Holy Spirit to help guide you ◆

Why Speak in Tongues?

What is significant about praying in tongues? Why is it so important that we speak in tongues?

When the Spirit of the Lord prays in other tongues through us, He places us on a different frequency than the devil. We are on a direct line of communication with our Heavenly Father that the enemy cannot decipher. We "bypass" Satan's radar!

Praying in the Spirit enables us to pray for healing and deliverance, and the devil doesn't know how to direct his attack! In I Corinthians 13:1, Paul said, "Though I speak with the tongues of men and the tongues of angels," the literal translation says, "the language of heaven." "Though I speak with tongues and I speak with the language of heaven."

In other words, sometimes we pray in our natural language, but then there are times when we're fighting against warring spirits or have so many distractions that we need to clear the air. That is when we need to switch frequencies and begin praying in the Holy Ghost. We need to pray in the tongues of angels, in the language of heaven. When we pray in the Spirit we bypass the devil's radar and our prayers can't be interrupted or "shot down" by the enemy.

When we pray in the Holy Ghost, we build ourselves up in the Spirit; we build our resistance to sin, discouragement, and depression.

A new heart also will I give you, and a new spirit will I put within you: and I will take away the stony heart out of your flesh, and I will give you an heart of flesh.

And I will put my spirit within you, and cause you to walk in my statutes, and ye shall keep my judgments, and do them.

-Ezekiel 36:26-27

CHAPTER 6

Is the Holy Spirit still at work today?

If you look at today's news headlines, you might think God's presence has been lifted from this earth. Believers are persecuted around the world, God's established institution of marriage is being threatened, and immorality is running rampant.

But in the midst of it all, God is pouring out His Holy Spirit in the last days, just as Joel prophesied in Joel 2.

I believe that we're living in those last days and that the coming of the Lord is nearing.

As we see prophecies being fulfilled, we need to open our hearts and cry, "God pour out your Spirit more than ever."

God has given us a Comforter to equip us for warfare and to connect us to the very throne of heaven. Through the Holy Spirit, we have a language of praise and worship, intercession, power, and hope. We must teach our children the importance of this language.

> "And these words, which I command thee this day, shall be in thine heart: And thou shalt teach them diligently unto thy children, and shalt talk of them when thou sittest in thine house, and when thou walkest by the way, and when thou liest down, and when thou risest up" (Deuteronomy 6:6-7).

God has given us His Name, His Word, and His Spirit to overcome the power of the enemy. Today's culture is constantly speaking their language of fear, doubt, and hatred. It is critical that we allow the Holy Spirit to speak through us loudly and clearly!

Talk about what God means to you. Talk about how the Lord saved you and how He gave you a dream.

Talk to your children and grandchildren about how the Lord has blessed you, protected you, delivered you, healed you, encouraged you, and provided for you . . . then the next generation will know God and the power of His Holy Spirit.

Speak it! Proclaim it!

If you don't remember anything else about what you have read in this book, remember this . . . **when you get filled with the Holy Spirit, He is not out there . . . He is IN you!**

He is in you to comfort you! To encourage you! To protect you! To empower you to be bold and prepared to proclaim His truth to all you meet!